From the author of MOVE OVER, MOTHER GOOSE!

MOTHER RUTH'S RHYMES

Lyrical Finger Plays & Action Verses
For Fun Reinforcement of Concepts Across the Curriculum

By **Ruth I. Dowell**

Illustrated by Peggy Trabalka and Others

The author is available to conduct workshops and/or highlight sessions for local, state, regional and national early childhood or reading organizations. For information and brochure, please contact:

POLLYANNA PRODUCTIONS
PO Box 3222 • Terre Haute, IN 47803-0222
(800) 257-3286

3052 2369

Introduction *(Philosophy & Technique)*

*Most early childhood books **merely delight the EYE;** but, through fingerplays and song-like action verses, this book will especially delight the **EAR** and give teachers a fun, quick and easy way to enhance, enliven and reinforce concepts across the curriculum. It is especially-valuable for its unique ability to promote class cohesivness and performance even in the presence of wide-ranging abilities.*

In keeping with the character and style of MOVE OVER, MOTHER GOOSE, this companion book presents a lyrical flow of meaningful language that meets children head-on wherever they happen to be in the developmental process to stimulate language participation, creativity and self-esteem.

Since the book that doesn't get read and used is no better than the book that doesn't get written, the primary goal here was that the material be consistent with and profoundly relevant to the experience and interest levels of children. In order to promote expressive language and articulation skills, *ease of verbalization* was written into the lines. This involved the use of rhythmic patterns of speech and movement that children instinctively enjoy.

Then, look for short *"phrase bites"* that encourage fluency in reading through the use of natural pauses, as in

"Prairie Dog." The technique of *cluster phrasing* has been utilized to further encourage greater fluency in oral expression and reading. Don't be shocked to see a series of words run together. These are not typographical errors, but simply a device to indicate the pace and flow of the word group. You'll discover this in a rhyme such as "Alameda Cheetah," where, "...want to meet a cheetah" becomes *"wannameetacheetah."* Occasionally, as few as two words will be involved; i.e., in "Big Ducks, Little Ducks," *"comeout to sun"* gives the reader or reciter the syncopated feel of the line that is essential to its rhythmic pattern. Since the latter cluster phrase is a closer equivalent to conversational speech, its encounter becomes even more gratifying, memorable and significant in the language development process.

The charm of these fresh, new finger plays and action verses will appeal to all children. Their regular use will contribute substantially to the versatility, effectiveness and professional satisfaction of both early childhood and elementary classroom teachers.

Animals & Other Friends

Familiar Experiences

Feelings

Humor and Nonsense

Seasons and Weather

Sharing

Shelter

Special Days

Town & Country

Transportation

The Universe & Me

Final Thought

Have you ever seen a zebra:
In the jungle or the zoo?
You can always tell a zebra
By his stripes and color, too.

Animal Population
Hereabouts

Birds	Manatee
Badger	Monkeys
Bear	Octopus
Camel	Ostrich
Caterpillar	Oysters
Cats	Pelican
Cheetah	Pig
Critter (Chipmunk)	Platypus
Deer	Porcupine
Ducks	Possum
Elephant	Prairie Dog
Ferret	Puma
Fish	Rhinoceros
Giraffe	Seal
Grasshoppers	Skunk
Hamster	Spider
Hippopotamus	Squirrel
Hyena	Swan
Iguana	Tarantula
Koala	Tiger
Leopard	Walrus
Lightning Bug	Whale
Lion	Wolf
Llama	Zebra

At the Zoo

Elephant, pelican, lion and bear;
Zebra, giraffe and the monkeys are there.
Now, look around at the people like you,
Visiting animal friends at the zoo.

Zebra

Have you ever seen a zebra
In the jungle or the zoo?
You can always tell a zebra
By his stripes and color, too.

Mr. Giraffe *ACTION RHYME*

(Children standing)

Point to leg	Mr. Giraffe, your legs are long;
Point to neck& nod	And, yes, your neck is, too!
Scratch head	Is there an animal anywhere
Hold hand high	That's quite as tall as you??

Alameda Cheetah

I went down to Alameda
where I heard they had a cheetah
and I got to meetacheetah
at the Alameda Zoo.
If you wannameetacheetah,
just go down to Alameda.
There's an Alamedacheetah waiting
just...for...you!

Petaluma Puma

I went up to Petaluma
where I heard they had a puma
and I got to petapuma
at the Petaluma Zoo.
If you wannapetapuma,
just go up to Petaluma.
There's a Petalumapuma waiting
just...for...you!

Leopard

A leopard is spotted or sometimes is black.
What*ever* his color is, don't turn your back!

Lion *FINGER PLAY*
(Children sitting)

Lean forward	A lion will look you
and tilt head	Right straight in the eye
Bring hands	And swallow your head,
together quickly	If your head is close by!

Cats! *FINGER PLAY*

(Children sitting)

Bring hands in/out	In they come, out they go!
Count on 2 fingers	Colored and calico!
Point to cat locations	Cats on the carpet and cats in the hall!
Motion in/out/in	In again, out again! Here they come in again!
Count 2 fingers	Colored and calico!
and hug self	I love them all!

Whale Tale

When a whale
Flips his tail,
You can get
Rather wet!

Feed the Fish

Don't forget to feed the fish,
Or how can they survive?
The food you feed the fish is all
That keeps the fish alive.

But please, don't feed the fish too much.
They eat and never stop,
Until one day you find the fish
All floating at the top!

Reggie Rhino ACTION RHYME

(Children standing)

Show arm muscles	Reggie Rhino! Whatta bozo!
Pull up from nose	Has a horn upon his nose-O!
Move elbows...	
and run in-place	Running, crashing through the jungle!
Shake finger	What a rude and rowdy fellow!

Thomas and Potomas

Thomas and Potomas live at the zoo:
A couple of hippos, and what do they do?
They swim and they splash in the pool; wouldn't you?
Thomas the Hippo and Potomas, too!

Elmo the Camel

Elmo the Camel has one hump, not two,
As some of his faraway relatives do.
He drinks just as much and he goes just as far
As all of his cousins, wherever they are!

Ostrich

Oh, an ostrich is a runner,
Running faster than a man;
Maybe faster than a camel
Or a race horse can!

And his feathers are so pretty
You can wear 'em on your hat.
But I wonder how you catch him
When he runs like that??

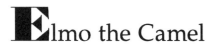

Oysters

Oysters in the sea,
 in the deep,
    cold
    sea.
Oysters in a bed
where they like
    to
    be.
Here comes a man
    in a boat
    with a net.
How many oys-ters
    will
    he
    get?

Oysters on-the-halfshell!
Oysters in the stew!
(*slower*) **If** *you* eat an oyster...,
(*faster*) **I** will eat one, *too!*

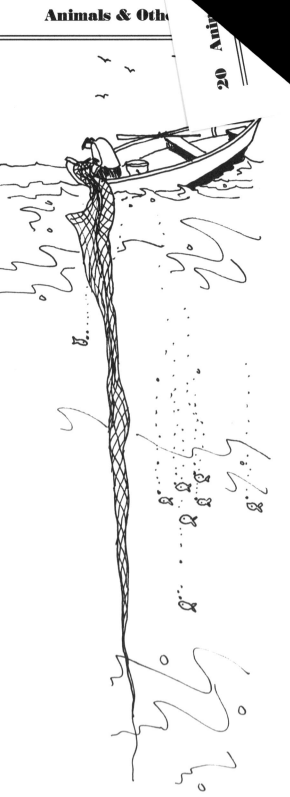

Hannah Hyena *FINGER PLAY*

(Children sitting)

Children nod heads	Hannah Hyena, you're homely, it's true.
"Giggle" behind hands	Do other animals make fun of you?
Frame face with hands	Bet you look fine to your mother and dad.
Clap hands	Parents are good about that: I'm glad!

Lone Wolf

Lone wolf howling in the dead of night.
I can see him in the pale moonlight.
Is he lonely? Has he lost his way?
Lone wolf waiting for the light of day.

Big Ducks, Little Ducks

Big ducks, little ducks swimming in the pond:
First, near the bank, then a little beyond.
Some ducks white and some ducks brown.
Tails go up when their heads go down!

Now, single file, as they comeout to sun:
Big ducks, little ducks, one-by-one.
Then said a duck with his feet still wet,
"One more thing: is it nap time yet?"

Big ducks, little ducks nestled in the grass.
Tiptoe lightly as you pass.

Ducks

When a duck takes a walk,
It's a *waddle*. When they talk,
It's a *"quack,"* not a *"cluck."*
That's the way you TELL a duck!

Mama Llama

(Say each line in a single breath.)

When a mama llama rocks a baby llama rock-a-by, *(breath)*
A mama llama sings a baby llama lullaby.

Porcupine

I wouldn't pet a porcupine,
Unless he was a friend of mine!

Skunk

A skunk is an animal I know quite well.
I don't often SEE one, but I smell his "smell!"

Ferret

If somebody gave you a ferret,
Would you eat it or pet it or wear it?

Swan

A swan a-swimming gracefully.
No sound I hear, but beauty see.

Iguana

I don't think I'd wanna
Pick up an iguana!

Seal

When a seal
Has a meal,
There's a fish
On his dish!

Walrus *ACTION RHYME*

(Children standing)

Shade eyes	I would like to see a walrus
Pull whiskers	With his whiskers long and stiff,
Hands under chin	See him resting on the seashore
Sniff the air	As he gives the air a sniff.
Move body vigorously	Would he wallow in the water,
Move body & arms	Splashing, splashing everywhere?
"Catch" a fish	Would he catch a fish and swallow it,
& swallow it	As if I weren't there?
Nod head	*Yes, he would!*

Millie Manatee

Millie Manatee eats only seaweed from the sea...
Not anything that swims. No fish for her...not she!
A grand and gentle creature where the ocean meets the shore:
She floats and bobs and dives until it's time to eat some more.

Deer

A deer was here!
It's very clear:
He never meant to stay.
He raised his head and sniffed the air
Then quickly went away.

At dusk or dawn he may come back
To have a look around;
And if he does, I'll hide myself
And make not any sound.

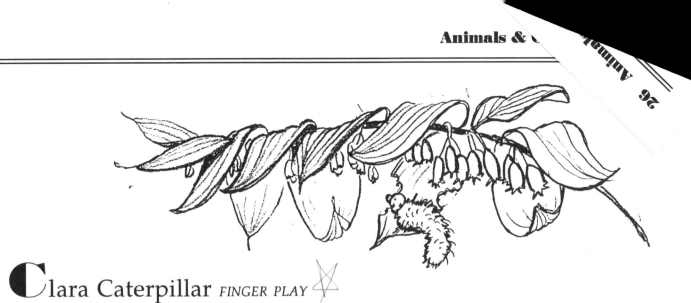

Clara Caterpillar FINGER PLAY

(Children sitting)

Shade eyes	I see Clara Caterpillar
Munch" fingers	Munching on a leaf.
Wiggle fingers down	Crawling on the topside,
Fingers still, pointed up	Hanging underneath.
Wiggle fingers	"Busy little wiggle worm,
Rub stomach	When you've had your fill,
	Will you stop and take a nap?
Lay face on hands	Of course, you will!"

Grasshoppers

Grasshoppers spit tobacco juice.
If you don't think it's true,
Just pick one up. He'll pucker up
And spitabit on you!

Possum in a Tree *FINGER PLAY*
(Children sitting)

Shade eyes	I see the moon.
Point to moon & self	The moon sees me.
Shade eyes again	We see a 'possum
	in a hol-low tree.
Look both ways	What do you see?
	A 'possum in a tree?
Nod head &	A 'possum in a tree
point to four fingers	with her fam-i-ly!

Mr. Koala

Mr. Koala,
Now, since you know alla
   the trees hereabouts, I've a hunch:
The one you like best
(*Eucalyptus*, I guess!)
   is the one where you're having your lunch!

Octopus and Platypus

The octopus said to the platypus, "Gee!"
Could you, by chance, be related to me?"
The platypus said, as he swam away,
(*Aussie accent*) "No...I'm not. No, I'm not:
No way!"

Critter in the Wood Stack

Critter in the wood stack
(maybe more than one!)
Underneath the kindling
Where I thought I saw him run!
If there's more than one
There could be even more than *three!*
"Little bitty critter, do you have a fam-i-ly?"

Scotty Squirrel *FINGER PLAY*

(Children sitting)

Run fingers up left arm	Up the tree the squirrel went
Repeat ...:	And faster down he came,
down right arm twice	With someone chasing after him
	And Scotty was his name!
Wrap arms around "tree"	"Scotty Squirrel **owns** the tree."
	That's what my parents say.
Wiggle fingers and hands	One thing's for sure:
	When strangers come,
quickly from l to r	He chases them away!

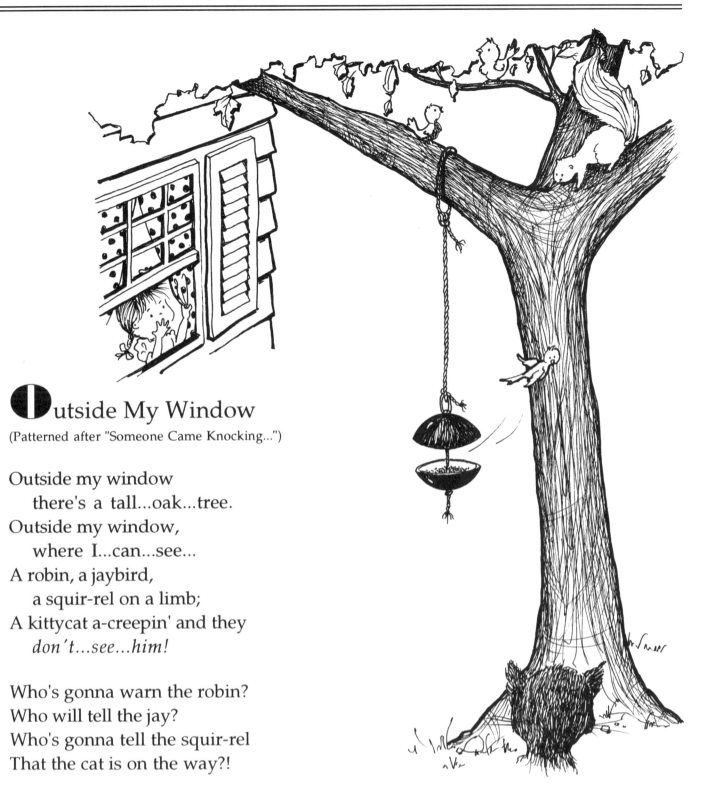

Outside My Window

(Patterned after "Someone Came Knocking...")

Outside my window
    there's a tall...oak...tree.
Outside my window,
    where I...can...see...
A robin, a jaybird,
    a squir-rel on a limb;
A kittycat a-creepin' and they
    don't...see...him!

Who's gonna warn the robin?
Who will tell the jay?
Who's gonna tell the squir-rel
That the cat is on the way?!

Open the bedroom window!
I see the pesky cat!
Shout from the bedroom window:
"Go away, Cat;
SCAT!"

Robin, I Say!

A bird
I heard
    in the yard
    on the fence
    has been there all morning
    and chir-ping since.

I know
    his name!
Here's how I can tell:
    I know by his song
    and his color, as well.

A redbird, a bluebird, a blackbird or jay?
Oh, no! It's a robin--*a robin*, I say!

Rodger the Badger

A tough little codger
Is Rodger the Badger!
He'll fight, if he has to, and win.
He'll win!
But, mostly he digs
And he claws and he scratches
For only the food he brings in.

Prairie Dog *ACTION RHYME*
(Children standing)

Hands overhead...	Prairie dog peekin' From a hole In the ground!
look around	Prairie dog lookin' All around, All around.
Shade eyes	What does he see; Maybe, what
Cup ears	Does he *hear?*
Stoop quickly	Pops back in Till the coast Is clear.

Spider *FINGER PLAY*
(Children sitting)

Fingers moving upward	Spider crawling on the wall,
Show "tiny"	Tiny body, legs and all!
Draw circle, both hands	Now I see the web you've spun.
Wipe brow	Was it work, or was it fun?

Tarantulas

I know a girl named Angela
Who has a pet tarantula.
She keeps it in a fancy pot
With bits of fruit and...*who knows what?!*

I don't like beetles, bugs and such
(Like other things that crawl!) that much.
So Angela will need to know
Her pet *or I* will have to go!

Hamilton Hamster

Hamilton Hamster, I know how you feel.
It must be quite boring all day on that wheel.
Now, would it be better (I think it *would* be)
If I could release you and you could run free??

Lightning Bug *FINGER PLAY*

(Children sitting)

Put fingers into palm	If I catch a lightning bug,
	I'll put him in a jar.
Spread fingers upward"	"Light up, little lightning bug,
	And show me where you are!"
	Said the little lightning bug,
Hands on hips	"That boy is back, I see!
Spread fingers upward	I'll shine my light
	No more tonight.
Hide behind hands	His jar will not get me!"

Oink LeBoink

Oink LeBoink, the Frenchman's pig,
He ate too much and got too big.
The Frenchman took him to the Fair.
He dropped him off and left him there.

The judges took one look at Oink
And said, "That pig is Oink LeBoink!"
They looked again with judges eyes
And gave that Frenchman's pig First Prize!

Close your eyes and make a wish
Swear you'll never tell!
If you've any, drop a penny
In the wishing well.

Did You Ever

Did you ever eat a snowball
    that you rolled up in your mitten,
    feel it cold against your teeth,
    inside your mouth? *(You sure you didn't?)*

Did you ever take a gallop
    high up on your daddy's back,
    holding tight and bouncing, bouncing,
    like a big potato sack?

Did you ever hold a puppy
    right up underneath your chin,
    feel the puppy cuddle closer,
    warm and wiggly? *Say when!*

Did you ever ride the "saddle"
    on your dad or grandpa's knee:
    "ride the horsey," like a cowboy?

Well, I did;
    so, lucky me!

Do It By Yourself

Did you use the toothpaste?
Did you put it back?
Did you hang your brush
    on the toothbrush rack?

Did you wash your hands?
Did you use the soap?
Did you wash your face
    and your ears, I hope!

Did you blow your nose?
Did you comb your hair?
Are you wearing pants, a shirt,
    your shoes and underwear?

You can go to school
When you've done all that.
Get your lunch, your gloves, your coat
And don't forget your hat!

Wait a minute! Wait a minute!
Never mind the fuss.
Pollyanna, now you've done it!
You have missed the bus!

I'm Rather Short *ACTION RHYME*

(Children standing)

Hold hand so high;	I'm rather short:
then higher	Not tall at all;
Spread arms wide	But give me room to grow,
Throw hand away from self	And in no time,
Point to self; hold hand high	I'll be as tall
Point to someone	As anyone you know!
Point to self; then, point finger	And when I am--yes!
Hold hand high	When I'm tall,
Point away; the, to self	They'll say to me,
Hand encircling mouth	*"Play basketball!"*
Extend right hand	And so he did!
Extend left hand	You may have heard.
Extend right hand	His name was Larry...
Extend left hand	Larry
Jumpshoot with right hand.	*Bird!*

SCORE

US   THEM

2   0

Setting the Table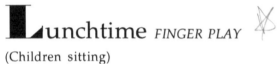

This is the way we set the table
Morning, night and noon:
Plate and napkin, cup and saucer,
Knife and fork and spoon.

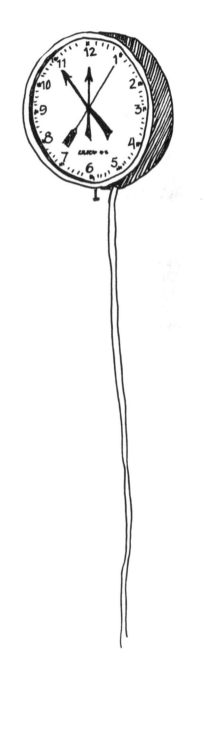

Lunchtime *FINGER PLAY*

(Children sitting)

Washing motion :	I'll wash my hands.
hands and face-	I'll wash my face.
Point to wrist	It's almost time for lunch.
Show "little bit"	I think I'll eat a *little bit*,
Spread arms wide	But I might eat *a bunch!*

Happy Time

Splashing in the water with a cup and a pan.
Fill it up and empty it? Yes, I can!

Digging in the dirt with a spoon and a spade.
Pile it high and pat it! See the hole I made?

Cutting with my scissors. Follow every line.
Paste it on the paper so it looks just fine!

Painting at the easel: yellow, green and blue.
Add a little red, now. That should do!

Dressing up a playtime. Resting when we should.
Doing things at school together sure feels good!

Close your Eyes

Close your eyes and make a wish.
Swear you'll never tell!
If you've any, drop a penny
In the wishing well.

In My Sandbox *FINGER PLAY*
(Children Sitting)

Dig with one hand	In my sandbox
	There's a spade,
Pick up bucket	Bucket,
Rake with fingers	Rake, and things
	I've made:
Count three things	Mountains, castles,
on fingers	Tunnels, too:
Hands up, over & down	Up and down,
Draw a circle	Around and
Palms together, hands	Through.
moving away from body.	

The Laundromat *FINGER PLAY*
(Children sitting)

Hold hand to ear	Hey, there, little girl: listen to that!
Move arms	*Your* mama's gonna go to the laun-dro-mat!
Curl fingers and	
drop in clothes	Gather up your dirty clothes. Put 'em in a sack.
Take hold of	
front of clothing	Everything's clean when your mama comes back!

The Laundry

Mother did the laundry;
Then she hung it out to dry.
Sleeves and legs and tops and things:
Patterns in the sky!

Overalls to underwear!
All hanging on the line.

Some are BIG
And some are not.
Guess
which
ones
are
mine!

Fishing

I caught a fish and it went flip-flop,
Right where it landed on the fish-ing dock!
Will we keep it? Will we not??
Fish flip-flopping on the fishing dock!

I Won't Have Fish

1-2-3-4-5! (clap, clap!) I caught a fish alive. (clap, clap!)
6-7-8-9-10 (clap, clap!) He got away again! Ohhhh...
What shall I eat today? (clap, clap!)
The fish has swum away! (clap, clap!)
I won't have fish!
The fish I wish
Went swish!
And swam away! (clap, clap!)

The Good Humor Man

Listen for the jingle of the
  ice
  cream
  van!
Everybody run
  to the "good
  humor man!"

"Popsicles, ice cream!
  Who
  wants
  some?"

"I do!" "I do!"
Yum, yum, yum!

Dreams Forgot

Sometimes I dream and sometimes not;
Or, is it that I just forgot?
Does morning come, as it would seem,
To light my brain, and steal my dream?

My Bubble Bath *FINGER PLAY*

(Children sitting)

Wiggle fingers	Bubbles in the water!
Form circle for "tub"	See the bubbles in the tub!
Smell hands	Lovely-smelling bubbles get me
Rub arms vigorously	Cleaner *when I scrub!*

Pancakes

When Mother makes us pancakes,
It's usually at night.
I know. They're good for breakfast;
But, that's all right.

Tonight, we're *having* pancakes.
I plan to eat a lot.
My brother thinks he'll eat the most;
But, I say, *maybe not!*

Lights Out! *FINGER PLAY*
(Children sitting)

Pull chain	Lights out! Pull the plug!
Pull covers up under chin	Under the covers as-snug-as-a-bug!
Hold eyes open with fingers;	If your eyes won't go to sleep,
then count on four fingers	Count the tails of fifty sheep.
Move fingers across body	If the sheep should run away,
Count on four fingers	Count their tails another day.

My Blanket

I once had a ba-by blan-ket.
My blan-ket was bright and new;
But...now...my...
Blan-ket is old and faded.
I wonderifyouhadablanket, too.
And...if...your...
Blank-et is old and faded,
Tattered and worn with time,
I...know...you...
Love that old blan-ket nearly
As much as I love mine!

If I'm naughty;
Then I'm nice,
Scold me once,
But hug me *twice*.

To Be Alone

Where can I go to be alone:
A nice little corner to call my own?
A cardboard box to crawl inside
Might be a place where I could hide;
Or, perched up high at the top of a tree,
Where, maybe, the leaves would cover me.
Or, walk through grass as high as my head.
Or, lie on my back in the grass instead.
Or, sit on the steps while cars whiz by
And count every one--at least, I'd try.

The monkey bars! A swinging gate!
Yes, time to be by yourself is great!
But always, when you come back home,
It's nice to know you're *not* alone.

Hands

FINGER PLAY
(Children sitting)

Praying hands	Hands are for praying
Extend hand;	And helping
then, cup it	And holding
Wave	And waving
and wash hands	And washing
Clap once;	And clapping...
Shake finger	*And scolding!*

Instead of Me

Sometimes I pretend to be
Someone else instead of me.
But only for a while and then
I'm BUSY BEING ME again.

How Old Are You? *FINGER PLAY*

(Children sitting)

	If you ask, "How old are you?"
Hold up two fingers	I will tell you, "More than two!
then, a third,	Count my fingers. Are there three?
a fourth and a fifth	Is that four or five you see?"

Someday, when I'm older, then

Hold up ten fingers   I could be as much as ten!

Hold up fingers for age   But right now, I'm THIS. I know

'Cause my mother told me so.

The Looking Glass

Looking in the looking glass,
And looking back at me
Is someone very special!
Here, you take a look and see!

Too Hard

You say, *"It's too hard!"*
You run off and hide.
You say, *"I can't do it!"*
But you haven't tried.

You'll learn to do things
That you see others do.
You're gonna be proud of
The person called, "You!"

And when you're all finished,
You feel oh-so-good;
And, that's when the teacher says
(*optional: "...your parents say..."*),
"I knew you could!"

Person Called, "You" *ACTION RHYME*

(Children standing in pairs)

Point to top of head	From the top of my head
Point to toes	To the tip of my toes;
(Repeat)	From my hat to my shoes
Move hand neck to ankles	In my in-between clothes,
Hold up one finger	There's a person called, "I."
Touch chest with both hands	There's a person called, "Me."
Point to self with one finger	I'm a "somebody"
Move hands away from each other in front of body	*Nobody else* can be!
Repeat gestures pointing to another person	From the top of *your* head
	To the tip of *your* toes;
	From *your* hat to *your* shoes
	In *your* in-between clothes,
Extend both hands to another	There's a person called, *"You."*
Hands on hips	Take a look and you'll see:
Nod head.	*You're* a **somebody**
	Nobody else can be!

When I'm a Little Older

(Tune: J. S. Bach Minuet in G)

When I'm a little **ol**-der
I **may** wanna be a **sol**-dier
Or **fly**
Like an eagle **high**
Way up in the **sky**
Where the planets **lie**;
Or, I
Could ride a circus **po**-ny
Or **float**
On a boat!
If **on**-ly
I **knew**
What I wanna **do**,
When I'm twenty-**two**,
When I'm old as **you**.

Tell Me a Story

Tell me a story, a scary one, please.
I like to be scared from my nose to my knees!
Then, tuck me in nicely and kiss me good night.
But, please leave a light...would you leave on the light?

Dragons! *ACTION RHYME*
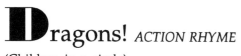

(Children in a circle)

Blow and move hands away	If you ever met a dragon,
	Breathing fire
"Wag" hand behind back end	And tail a-waggin',
Applaud	Do you think
	It would be fun;
Disperse and run away	Or, would you
	Turn around
	And run?!

Hug Me Twice

If I'm naughty, then I'm nice,
Scold me once, but *hug me twice!*

Inside My House

Inside my house, inside my room
I keep the things I treasure.
Inside my heart, inside my mind
My thoughts should give me pleasure.

And so, inside of all of these
I want what's best for me:
Not ugly things and angry thoughts.
They're not good company!

Looking Down

I climb up a ladder or climb up a tree
To look down at people, as they do at me.

All About Babies

How big is a baby?
Much smaller than I!
When babies get hungry,
That's when they cry.
They crawl everywhere
Till they learn how to walk
And make funny sounds
While they're learning to talk.
They sleep in a bed
With the sides pulled up high
And always wear diapers.
(I guess you know why!)

Babies are people
Beginning to grow.
I used to be one--
That's how I know.
And where do they come from?
I wish I knew!
Where did I come from;
And...where did **you**??

I'm Angry!

I'm angry! Yes, I'm angry!
And here's the reason why:
Somebody pushed me! Hit me!
And that can make you cry!

And when I'm angry, this is what
I always wanna do:
I wanna hit somebody back!
Do you feel that way, too?

But sometimes if I cry, it's 'cause
I'm feeling sick or sad.
So *many* things can happen that
Can make someone feel bad.

(And as for crying, it's okay.
It makes the feeling go away!)

If I Were Younger ACTION RHYME

(Tune: Tschaikowsky Violin Concerto)
(Children standing)

Rock a baby	If I were younger;
Show "small" with hands	If I were smaller;
Point to self	I would
	Be a
Rock a baby and nod	Baby; yes, I would.
Flash 10 fingers twice	If I were older,
Raise one hand, palm down	If I were bigger,
Point to self	I could
	Be a
Raise both hands over head	Grown-up. Yes, I could!
Point to self	But I
Rock a baby	Am neither;
	I am
Raise both hands over head	Not either.
Point to self	I am
	What I
Tap chest with both hands	Am and *who* I am!

Mary, be wary
Of crows and canaries!
They nest in your hair
Eating beetles and berries...

Ole! Hooray! Ole! *ACTION RHYME*

(Children standing)

Cup mouth	Ole! Hooray! Ole!
Dangle cape l & r	The bullfighter fights today!
Forefingers above head	The bull's in the ring--
	but hold everything!
Turn & run	The bullfighter went thataway.
	Ole!

Billy Deedy

(Take turns saying the following in one breath, if possible;
or use it as a 4-part round)

Billy Deedy wrote graffiti
On the wall and with his feet he
Made some prints upon the fence and
Signed his name.   His name is...

(repeat)

Trudy and Judy

Trudy and Judy, identical twins,
Look so much alike it confuses their friends.
Said Judy,"There's one way to tell who I am:
My sister likes jelly, while I prefer jam!"

Oops!

I once saw a man with a leaky umbrella,
Who said, "There's a hole in my old *underbrella.*"

There once was a boy running after a butterfly.
Then, what he said was, "I caught me a *flutterby.*"

Maybe tonight you'll be having spaghetti.
Don't make a mistake and say, "Pass the *pasghetti!*"

The Clothes Pin

Freddie found a clothes pin.
Stuck it on his nose.
Doesn't need a handkerchief,
Because he never blows!

Eddie Wears Overalls

Eddie wears overalls
Under his coveralls.
Under his overalls
   what does he wear??

Under his coveralls,
Under his overalls,
Eddie wears underwear
   under them all!

itten Mitten

If a kitten lost a mitten,
Could she knit another mitten?
Would the knitted kitten mitten
Match the mitten on her paws?

If a kitten lost a mitten,
No, she couldn't knit a mitten;
And the reason why she couldn't is:
Because...because...*because!*

r. Liddle *FINGER PLAY*

(Children sitting)

Prepare to play	Mr. Liddle had a fiddle.
Start playing	"Fiddle, Mr. Liddle, DO!"
Play faster	Faster, faster did he fiddle
Hold1 piece in each hand	Till he sawed the thing in two!

Eleven Young Ladies

Eleven young ladies had liver for lunch
And eight left it lay on the plate.
Said Young Lady Nine, "I'll eat all of mine."
Said Ten and Eleven, "That's great! We'll wait!"

Mary, Be Wary

Mary, be wary of crows and canaries.
They nest in your hair, eating beetles and berries.
They chirp and they burp and they drive you berserk!
So, Mary, remember: be wary!

The Puppet

(Tune: Irish Jig)

They painted the flagpole.
The puppet went up it.
Now, which has more paint?
Does the pole or the puppet?

The pole had more paint
Till the puppet went up.
Now, would you believe,
All the paint's on the puppet!

Inside a Sack

Apple Jim and Apple Jack,
Side-by-side inside a sack,
Shouted out, "Hooray! Hooray!
We get to go to school today!"

If I Had Five Eyes
(Tune: "A Comedy Tonight" from
Something Happened on the Way to the Forum)

If I had five eyes,
If I had three knees,
If I had yellow elbows,
Would you mar-ry me?

"If you had six lips;
If they were all blue;
If you had purple urples,
I would marry you!"

Leon *FINGER PLAY*
(Children sitting)

Pretend to chew toes:	Leon chewed on all his toes:
Left ones,	All of these
Then right ones	And all of those!
Hold out hands& shrug	Why he did it, no one knows.
Hold stomach	He was hungry, I suppose.

Wheels for Feet

If I had wheels instead of feet,
I think it might be kinda "neat"
To roll all over everywhere
And always be the first one there!

But, when it came to time for bed,
I'd wish that I had feet instead.
Imagine! Underneath your sheet
A pair of wheels instead of feet!

The Punkin' Patch

If you smiled at a punkin' in a punkin' patch,
Would the punkin' in the punkin' patch...
Smile back??

Uncle Eatsomore

Hide the crackers! Hide the cheese!
Hide the biscuits--hurry, please!
Can the fruit and freeze the meat!
Stash it, if it's good to eat!

Lock the cupboard! Hide the key!
Put it where no one can see!
Close the windows! Bolt the door!
Here comes Uncle EATSOMORE!

■ I like Winter.
I like Spring.
I like the Summer
When the birdies all sing....

Seasons of the Year

(Tune: "I like coffee, I like tea...")

I like Winter. I like Spring.

I like the summer when the birdies all sing.

Winter and Spring, Summer and Fall.

What is *your* favorite season?

I like them ALL!

Spring!

This is Spring! I know it well:
The look, the feel, the sound...the smell
Of flowers blooming everywhere,
As bunnies boldly sniff the air.

The songs of birds that dot the trees
Among the newly-clustered leaves;
And, there's the sun so warm and bright!
There's no mistake: It's Spring, all right!

Under the Umbrella

Under the umbrella, out in the rain.
If it should thunder, go back in again.
Thunder and lightning: I hear, I see.
"Thunder and lightning, you don't scare me!"

Umbrella People

Under a thundering, rumbling sky,
People with umbrellas hurrying by.
Clouds like the smoke from a steam engine train,
Waiting for thunder to shake out the rain.

Wind! *FINGER PLAY*

(Children sitting)

Make sound of wind	I can hear the wind blow,
Move head left to right	Rushing by my window.
Touch finger to forehead	Wonder where the wind goes??
Hands up and moving	*Ev-ry-where!*
Draw trees	Up among the tree tops,
Dangle fingers	Down upon the housetops.
Touch finger to forehead	Wonder where the wind stops??
Point twice	*It's there!*
Hold tight to lunch pail	Pulling at my lunch pail;
Pull on back of shirt	Snapping at my shirt tail;
Make a triangle	Filling up a boat sail:
Shake finger twice	*That's where!*

Summertime

In the summer
   you can swim
   in a lake
   or the sea.
You can camp
   in a tent
   or your own RV.

You can even
   take a trip
   on a plane,
   in a car.
In the summer
   life is great
   anywhere you are!

Batter Up!

Danny hung his jacket
On a wooden picket fence.
He swung the bat; the umpire said:
"Now let the game commence!"

The first pitch was a "sinker."
Said Dan, "That's not my style."
The second was a fast ball and
He hit the thing a mile!

It's nice to be a hero and to
Hear your teammates roar.
And on this day the home team beat
The visitors by four!

Autumn

Autumn means
Falling leaves,
Haunted places,
Scary faces,
Window soaping,
Chimney smoking,
Colder weather,
Nuts to gather.
Summer's gone:
We're movin' on!

Wintertime *FINGER PLAY*

(Children sitting)

Point to toes and nose	Tingly toes and a ro-sy nose!
Take hold of ear lobes	Stinging ears
	When the cold wind blows!
"Close door"	Betterclosethehouse
	up tight before...
March in-place	Wintertriestomarch
	in through the door!

Snow on the Housetop *ACTION RHYME*

(Children standing)

Fingers high and bobbing	Snow on the housetop.
Move hands across body	Snow on the ground.
Wiggle fingers downward	Snow in the air,
	coming down,
	coming down.
Zip up coat	Puton your coat,
Hold out hands and tip hat	Your gloves and hat.
Shovel twice	Shovelofftheside-walk:
	like that!

Look Out the Window! *ACTION RHYME*

(Children standing)
Tune: Up on the Housetop

Shade eyes	Look out the window! See the snow!
Point to:	Coat and hat and gloves, let's go!
Measure boot top	Up to my boot tops on the ground!
Show shape	Let's make a snowman, fat and round!
Point l & r	I'll do this, and you do that.
Shake finger	Don't forget:
Touch top of head	He needs a hat.
Touch each:	And now, comes the nose, the mouth and eyes.
Shade eyes	Look out the window:
Mouth open, eyes wide	*Sur-prise!*

I have two and you have none.
If I share, we each have one.
Should I share? I guess I should...
Just the way I know you would.

Sharing

"Sharing" is a word I learned
When I was only two.
So I've had lots of practice
With my fam'ly, haven't you?

Only One Piece *FINGER PLAY*

(Children sitting)

Hold up one finger	Only one more piece of pie.
Point to another, then self	Who should have it: you or I?
Finger to forehead	Think a minute...what to do.
Extend left, then right hand	*"Half for me, and half for you!"*

About Sharing *FINGER PLAY*

(Children sitting)

Hold up two fingers	I have two
Thumb to finger	And you have none.
Hold up one finger	If I share,
on each hand	We each have one.
Touch finger to forehead	Should I share?
Nod head	I guess I should:
Reach out with hand	Just the way
	I know *you would!*

Neighbors

It's nice to look across the fence
And see your neighbor there,
Especially if he's holding up
A brand new toy to share!

High in a Tree

High in a tree, where a squirrel has a nest,
An old crow named Jim stopped to take him a rest.
"I've been lotsa places and seen things," he said;
"But now, I need someplace to lay down my head."

He measured the nest with a glance of his eye
And said, "It's just right for a bird such as I."
He ruffled his feathers; he snuggled his beak.
This weary old crow hasn't slept for a week!

But two trees away on a sassafras limb,
I hear someone chattering. Does he see Jim?
And if he sees Jim, will he chase him away.
Or, what do you think? *Will he just let him stay??*

The Apple Tree *FINGER PLAY*
(Children standing)

Hold palms up	Under the apple tree
Look around	I'll look around.
on the ground	There may be a juicy one
Pick up apple	Here on the ground.
Pick up another	And if I get lucky
Hold up both	And find there are two,
Rub apples on shirt	I'll polish them nicely
Give one away	And give one to you.

Nellie Had an Apple

Nellie had an apple
And the apple had a worm.
When she took a bite
She saw the apple worm *squirm!*

Will she eat the apple?
Will she throw it out the door?
SHE could eat the apple, and
The WORM could have the CORE!

The Secret

(Activity: Children standing in a row whisper secret message from one person to the next. Last person reveals "secret." Object: To compare original "secret" with the one at the end of the line.)

I know a little secret.

Let me whisper it to you.

A secret isn't fun without

Someone to tell it to.

So now, you know my secret;

And, of course, you'll want to find...

Another ear to whisper in;

And no, I wouldn't mind.

The roof I live under
Is shelter to me.
Not a nest nor a hive,
'Cause I'm not a bee....

I Live in a House *FINGER PLAY*

(Children sitting)

Point to ceiling	The roof I live under
Hands over head	Is shelter to me.
Cup hands	Not a nest,
Make oval shape	Nor a hive,
Point to self	'cause I'm not a bee!
Point to shoe	Not like the "old lady
	Who lived in a shoe."
"Draw" house	I live in a *house!*
Point to another	Prob -ly you do, too.

If I Lived

If I lived
In a shack,
In an old RV;
If I lived
In a tent,
Would you vi-sit me?

Listen, Friend;
Don't you know
I would still be there
If you lived
In a cave
With a grizz-ly bear!

Where Do You Live? *ACTION RHYME*

(Children standing)

Point to "ground"	Do you live in the ground?
Show shapes	In a barn, in a tree?
Draw trees	Do you live in the woods
	Where the rent is free?
Point to "ground"	Said the worm,
	"In the ground,
	Not a house like you."
Draw a tree	"In a tree," said the bird,
Flap arms	And away he flew.
Draw a barn	"In a barn," said the cow.
Draw trees	"In a woods," said the bear.
Point to someone	Do you live in a trailer?
	In a tent?
Cup mouth	*Say where!*

My House *FINGER PLAY*

(Children sitting or standing)

"Draw" a house,	The house that I live in
Small rectangle	Has windows
And large rectangle	And doors,
Point to furniture,	Rooms full of furniture,
ceiling and floor	Ceilings and floors;
Make triangle overhead	A roof with a chimney,
Then, palms down	A porch with a screen.
Draw/color with fingers	I'll draw you a picture.
	You'll see what I mean.

My Room

Mother says my room's a mess.
Who should clean up? Take a guess!.
Picking up is such a chore!
Maybe I'll just close the door.

My Treehouse *FINGER PLAY*

(Children sitting)

Palms up,	If it should rain
...testing for rain	And catch me here
Point to feet	Without my boots
	And rainday gear,
Make triangle overhead	I wonder if
	My treehouse roof
Shake clothes	Would keep me dry?
with fingertips,,	To tell the truth
	It's rather old;
	And, now and then,
Palms up, testing	I've felt the rain
"Drip" with fingers	Come dripping in.
Make shape for "sun"	But, see the sun?
Shake head	No rain today!
Cross arms	And here I am,
	So here I'll stay?

Special Days

This is someone's birthday
Can you tell me who?
I've a certain feeling
That it could be you...!

Birthday Party!

It's a party! Big surprise!
Can't believe it? Rub your eyes!

Birthday person, proud and tall!
"Happy birthday!" sing we all!

Should we paddle? Yes or no.
Four times, five times, six or so?

Lots of presents! Boxes, bows!
What's inside, do you suppose??

Pretty candles on a cake!
How many candles did it take?

Everybody find a seat.
Ice cream's melting! Come and eat!

Birthday Spanks

When your birthday comes,
And they're handing out spanks,
If you want 'em, say *"Please."*
If you don't: *"No, thanks!"*

Someone's Birthday

(Activity: *Class says first six lines.*
Birthday person says the last six.)

This is someone's birthday.
Can you tell me who?
I've a certain feeling
That it could
   be
   you!

"Yes, it IS my birthday.
I'm the one, all right!
Will you want to paddle me?
   I think
   you
   might!"

alentine

Did you find a valentine
In your paper sack?

Did it say, "I love you,"
And things
Like
That?

Was there one from someone
That didn't
Say
Who?

Did you know I sent that valentine
To
You?

Off to the Zoo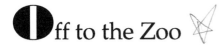

Fasten your seat belt! We're off to the zoo!
We've packed enough food *for the animals, too!*
Some nuts, a banana, a basket of hay;
A chunk of raw meat and a carrot bouquet!

Now, won't it be fun, as we're eating our lunch,
To sit on a bench while the animals munch?!
Then, Uncle Sylvester said, "Stop where you are!
You can't feed the animals! *Unload the car!"*

"Why, don't you remember? The sign at the zoo
Says, 'Don't feed the animals!' Here's what to do:
Just take out the hay and the chunk of raw meat;
And leave all the rest for the children to eat."

(They didn't eat hay nor the chunk of raw meat;
So, what did they take for the children to eat??)

The Parade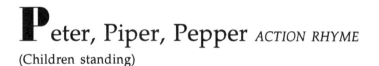

Hats off! Hear the drum!
Down the street the marchers come!
Pick me up and hold me high.
Now, I see them passing by!

Peter, Piper, Pepper ACTION RHYME
(Children standing)

Beat the drum	Peter has a bass drum.
Play the flute	Piper has a flute.
Blow the horn	Pepper has a brass horn:
	Tootely-toot-toot!
March in a circle	Peter, Piper, Pepper,
	Going down the street!
	Everybody marching
	To the beat, beat, beat!

Walking through the pasture!
Running down the path!
Jumping in the pond!
Whatta way to take a bath...!

Uptown, Downtown

Uptown, downtown, riding all around town!
Do you have a hometown?
Say where!

Uptown, downtown, riding all around town!
Yes, I have a hometown:
(Name your city.)

The City

If you ever go to town,
Stop and take a look around.
There's a sidewalk for your feet.
Cars and buses use the street.
Traffic lights are always flashing.
(That's to keep the cars from crashing!)
Buildings reach up to the sky,
Holding stores with things to buy.

It's a busy place to be:
That's "the city!" Go and see!

The Farm

Raccoon in the corn patch! Rabbit in the peas!
Robin stealing cherries and the dog a-scratchin' fleas!
Papa on the tractor. Mama in the house.
Tabitha the Cat playing "Gotcha!" with a mouse.

Little Boy Drew *FINGER PLAY*

(Children standing)

"Come" motion	Little Boy Drew,
	Come plant some corn.
Look at wrist	The farmer is waiting...
	He's waited since morn.
Show cornstalks	After the corn reaches
	Up to the sky,
Scarecrow stance	Make sure the scarecrow
	Is standing by!

Crows Don't Crow

(Activity: *Teacher/Class Language Interaction*)

A duck goes, *"Quack!"*
And a bee goes, *"Buzz!"*
Crows don't crow, *"but a rooster does!"*
A pig goes, *"Oink!"*
And a cow goes, *"Moo!"*
How does a rooster go? *"Cockadoodle doo!"*
A chick goes, *"Chirp!"*
As a fly flies by. (Children flap arms)
Crows don't crow. *"I can tell you why!"*
A hen goes, *"Cluck!"*
And a cat, *"Meow."*
Crows don't crow *"...'cause they don't know how!"*

The Pond

Walking through the pasture!
Running down the path!
Jumping in the pond:
Whatta way to take a bath!

Splashing like a whale!
Diving like a duck!
Someone sits a-fishing:
"Are you having any luck?"

Fingers getting wrinkled.
Lips are getting blue.
Time to get on home, now.
Let's do!

Butterfly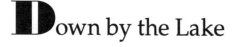

I can be a butterfly.
See me as I flutter by!
Rainbow wings,
Such dusty things,
Powdering the sky.

Down by the Lake

Down by the lake, camping out one day,
Bugs were biting!
"Get the can! Get the spray!"

"Flee!" said the fly. Said the flea, *"Me, too!"*
So they jumped and they flew: twenty-three *skidoo!*

Transportation

I'd like to ride the horsey,
But the horse won't go;
And even if he would,
I think he'd go too slow....

Take a Ride

You can ride IN a wagon, IN a car, IN a van.
You can ride IN a boat, IN a buggy: YOU CAN!
Take a ride ON a train, ON a horse, ON a bike.
If you don't take a ride, you can take a hike!

If you don't take a hike and you do take a ride,
Are you IN?? Are you ON?? Stop and think.

DECIDE!...

(sled skateboard airplane truck pony spaceship, etc.)

The Hayride

Hitch up the horses! Let's go for a ride!
Climb in the wagon, up over the side.
Down in the valley, a fire burning bright.
Marshmallows, hot dogs! A hayride tonight!

Up the River *ACTION RHYME*

(Children standing)

Rock back & forth	Up the river in a boat.
	Hope the old boat stays afloat!
Paddle l. & r.	Oars are dipping left and right.
	Won't be home till late tonight!
Hands at sides	Trees on both sides tall and green.
Fingers touching overhead	Sun a-shining hot and mean!
Splash water on self	Water splashing head to feet!
Paddle home	Let's go home! It's time to eat!

One Flies High

Helicopter! Air-plane!
Up in the sky!
One flies low and
One flies high.

Now, on the run-way
Side-by-side.
Helicopter! Air-plane!
Choose and ride!

Fasten your seat-belt!
Here we go!
Climbing! Climbing!
Look below:

Fields and farms!
So much to see!
Back to the air-port.
Landing! Wheee...!

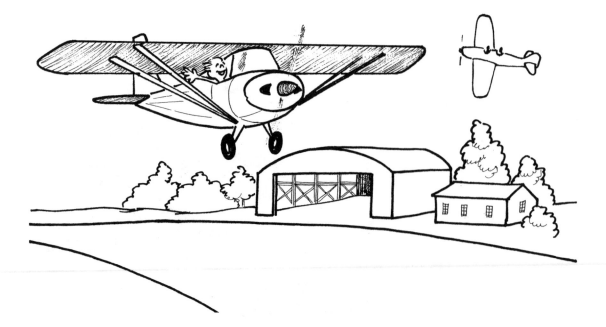

Train on the Track

(Follow the leader, with children reciting as they move about the room)

Clickety clack!
Train on the track!
Whereisitgoingandwillitcomeback?
Big...black
Train on the track!
Clickety, clickety,
Clickety, *clack!*

(repeat as desired)

Herbert the Hobo

Herbert the Hobo, he hopped on a train
And lived in a boxcar from Georgia to Maine.
They didn't collect and he didn't pay rent.
He followed the engine wherever it went.

He headed for Georgia when cold weather came.
In summer you'd find him away up in Maine.
He must have been happy; I don't know why not.
He never got cold and was never too hot!

The Carousel *ACTION RHYME*

(Children standing in a circle)

Holding hands..   I'd like to ride the horsey,
But the horse
Won't
Go!
Move   And even if he would,
around   I think he'd go
circle   Too
slowly   Slow.

Touch forehead   I know what I can do:
I'll buy a ticket!
So can you!...

Move quickly   And ride a horsey very well
around circle   Around the car-ou-sel!

The Universe & Me

Is there a place in outer space
...where I might like to go...?

The Nearest Star

The sun, they say, is our nearest star.
I wonder how far all the other stars are??
So far, that a twinkle is all you can see.
As far as *forever*, the stars seem to be!

Count All the Stars

Count all the stars--all the fish in the sea.
Count all the people, and don't forget me!
More than all my fingers. More than all my toes.
More than I can count, *and more than anyone knows!*

Outer Space

Is there a place
In outer space
With sun and rain and snow;
With lots of trees
And falling leaves,
Where I might like to go?

Or, is it just another place
I've never gone to see,
Where on one is or ever was
And wouldn't want to be?

It's far away; so, not today.
Tomorrow? *Maybe so!*

Wheels and Handlebars

I'd like to go to the moon *(oh, yes!)*
Or take a trip to Mars;
But that's for *astronauts.* I'm stuck
With wheels and handlebars!

Sunset *FINGER PLAY*

(Children sitting)

Touch fingers for "sun"	I have seen the sun
Slowly lower "sun"	Go down,
	As day turns into night.
Quickly cover eyes	*Peek-a-boo!* And then it's gone:
	Completely out-of-sight!
Touch fingers for moon	And I've watched
Slowly raise "moon"	The full moon rising,
	Knowing men have traveled there,
	Seen it moving
	like a spaceship
Float hands	On its way to
	...who-knows-where!

About the Planets *FINGER PLAY*

(Children sitting)

Cup left ear	I hear about the planets
Extend arms skyward	Up there in outer space.
Cup right ear	I hear about the moon, and yet
Cup face	I only see its face.
Tap forehead	While mostly I believe the things
Cup ear	I hear
Touch forearm	And touch
Shade eyes	And see,
Hold chin in hand	There must be more to learn about
Place hands on chest	The Universe...***and me***

How I Wonder!

How I wonder as I ponder
Things around me that astound me.
As I wonder, see me growing.
See me learning, doing, *knowing!*

Don't Open the Door!

Tune: Rock-a-my Soul

Whatta you do, when the wind is blowing 'round?
Whatta you do, when the lightning lights the town?
Whatta you do, when the rain is comin' down?
"Don't open the door!"

Whatta you do, if the wolf should huff and puff?
Whatta you do, if the goin's gettin' rough?
Whatta you do, if the wolf says, "Had enough?"
"Don't open the door!"

Whatta you do, when you hear a scary sound?
Whatta you do, when your heart begins to pound?
Whatta you do, when a stranger comes around?
"Don't open the door!"

Rock-a-my soul in the bosom of Abraham!
Rock-a-my soul in the bosom of Abraham!
Rock-a-my soul in the bosom of Abraham!
Ohhh, rock-a-my soul!